# Tunnel

*New Women's Voices Series No. 176*

*poems by*

# Lisa Furmanski

*Finishing Line Press*
Georgetown, Kentucky

# Tunnel

## ACKNOWLEDGMENTS

Tunnels: Oldupai Gorge, Tunnels: Perennial Bed: *Gettysburg Review*
Allium, The Quarry, Wintering: *Prairie Schooner*
When Wolf: *Tupelo Quarterly*
Laid Down in the Garage with a Gun: *Cimarron Review*
Blow, Water in the Well the Girl is Down: *Western Humanities Review*
When Coleoptera, When Backlit: *The Massachusetts Review*
When Alpine: *Hunger Mountain*
The History of Mothers of Sons: *Poetry*
Tunnels: Perennial Bed was featured on the *Poetry Daily* website.
While She Was Spinning was commissioned for the Norwich Historical
Society.
Pairings from V*ows a*re based on photographs from Unlikely Friendships
by Jennifer S. Holland.

Publisher: Leah Huete de Maines
Editor: Christen Kincaid
Cover Art: Joanne Hayes
Author Photo: Kata Sasvari
Cover Design: Elizabeth Maines McCleavy

Order online: www.finishinglinepress.com
also available on amazon.com

Author inquiries and mail orders:
Finishing Line Press
PO Box 1626
Georgetown, Kentucky 40324
USA

# Table of Contents

Tunnel: Oldupai Gorge ......................................................... 1

Tunnel: The Front ............................................................... 2

Tunnel: Tioga County .......................................................... 3

Tunnel: Perennial Bed .......................................................... 4


ONE

Princess Leia ..................................................................... 6

Water in the Well the Girl is Down ...................................... 8

The Quarry ....................................................................... 9

Ardors for the Lepidopterist ............................................. 10

When Backlit .................................................................. 12

Killer Selfies ................................................................... 13

When Wolf ..................................................................... 14

Blow ............................................................................... 15

When Original ................................................................ 16

While She Was Spinning .................................................. 17

The Girl in the Cupboard ................................................. 19


TWO

The History of Mothers of Sons ........................................ 22

Vows .............................................................................. 23

When Coleoptera ............................................................ 25

Allium ............................................................................ 26

When Alpine ................................................................... 27

Lay Down in the Garage with a Gun .................................. 28

How We Were at the End of Winter ................................... 30

Wintering ....................................................................... 32

When Crow ..................................................................... 33

## Tunnel:  Oldupai Gorge

My life was never gentle,
yet here you are

with brushes & cloth
dusting molars.
Prying the flint flake
from my fingers.

Swept-up shards, less complete
than a pot or axe
with no moorings of flesh to fail.

Millennia blanket my vertebrae,
a brooding way to lose the sky,
and yes, there was a final grain
that cinched the dark.

Then the desolation
of lying beyond the reach
of another, her marrow
too soft to last.

Beetles roam my clavicles,
collapsing into lines,
urging seepage & tectonics:
surface us.  You wonder

if my girlhood split,
what I sacrificed for dust.
You too are relic and
already know.  You,

whose neck freckles
& peels despite a soft hat,
you who thrills
at my pelvis in your palm.

## Tunnel: The Front

Your skull is a bowl of sound: spoon-scrape & jack-kick.

The tunnel roof your helmet tongues, strap at your chin,
months spent lying on top of your heart.

Air shared, lung to lung, like a single scoop
of earth, passed down the line, a small mound at the mouth.

Open space is claustrophobic, too much infinity in a way.

There should always be a pebble
pressed into a rib, each breath dented by its tiny heft.

Something to push against with mere mouthfuls.

You left sweat & piss & hair & spit, as dormant as coal.
Your nights shudder, tethered to echoes,

and you mine the sheets for lives you shed there.

## Tunnel: Tioga County

Where coal grows, our tunnel
divines it, our lamps dragging moons
over seams & veins.

The light snapped off its source and portered
down like a sacrificial girl,
to the subterranean where
there are no themes for beauty.

We were not always blind,
groping the faults, smelling where to dig.
Plummeting this shaft
instead of wrestling straw.

Either path chokes, our breath caked
with air & what is not air:
black damp that snuffs the bird.

Our tunnels do not break
out to the sky, each inch drills deeper.
The tunnel is not a passage,
mining cannot make it so.

## Tunnel: Perennial Bed

Carbon is eternal,
but soil is a dead thing,
black crescents
under my nails.

Moles, with thumbs
for lips & blind bodies,
store poison in their skin
and are inedible.

Claustrophobia,
a cenozoic unease,
is more than a worm
in a tunnel that silhouettes
the worm,
but my dream
of vanishing
inside my shadow.

A worm is perfect
prey, eyeless & legless.
Pink rings pressed against
the mole's star-nose,
then on the tongue
cradled in its jaws.

The garden breathes,
softened by diggers that skirt
bulbs & roots, dangling
like great chandeliers.

My trowel blade descends
like lightning,
a blinding rip of sky.

# ONE

## Princess Leia

When I go missing from
                 my childhood, Leia beams

her blue whisper
                 out of a red eye. You are

my only hope.  Who haunts who
                 when neither of us

is manifest in her body?
                 Every year

for seven years, my hair in wheels
                 (my mother's mouth

of metal pins), a loose sheet belted.
                 *Trick or treat!*

Other children with idle threats,
                 I was not that kind

of child:  never idle, always faithful
                 to threat. She

never believed I was Leia,
                 saber of cardboard, scribbled

trigger.  Holed up—a subdivision parroting
                 every other division—

nights ran blue and she ignored the door bell.
                 Strictly, it ended:

childhood, photographs, any mix of mirth
                 and light.  Every ritual

I should know (hallows
          and hosannas) was nixed,

no pulpy rites for carving teeth,
          and sequels

that might have echoed do not.  How
          can I grip

one like Leia, made entirely
          of glow?  I cannot.

And that red eye? No hope at all.

## Water in the Well the Girl is Down

At the taste of my rust she puckers,
though she sips deep.

Silt of the water tables, flowing bits
of hair, a cold velvet,
which her bloodedness cannot bear.

She dips a finger lacily and hums old hums:
a sable horse to plunge down, a cherry branch
to haul her up.

Tears, her water in mine, droplets intact
as long as I resist,
yet my wet craves salt.

Doubt is the disk of sky
at the opening of the well,
how brutal it is
that she saccades with the moon.

She outgrows
her pinafore, a fine frost shines her scalp, toes
gone to the rats.

Still, she is
what my body makes her,
solid and distinct.

I could float
her head upwards, lips bubbling,
hair a-swirl,

or slowly grind
the stones, lower the well so she rises.

And steps outside
her truth, homing to some other's will.

The girl is flimsy, plain as can be.

## The Quarry

Eventually, I would flip the shell to see, though blessed
with bony carapace, where her dampness dragged behind,

coital streaks through an arcade of tall, slow grass,
and would imagine a male in pursuit along a tether

between the soft and the rigid—a ritual
that could not close, the lush vulnerability

that is so typical of women.  And I would stop
speaking kindly, cased in my father's shirts, and feed

the turtle its ground meat and bone.
And this pet, twenty years later, from her shell

would not emerge, despite dunking under a cold tap.
Another twenty years, and my shadow is stuck

on hands and knees, lowering a box into a hole.
A girl can harden, hearing the nocturnal clanks

of a creature trying to climb glass.

## Ardors for the Lepidopterist

In the vacant lot, I swoop
my net on a cat-tail where matched wings fan,
careful not to rip the iridescence.

Lower the killing jar,
and a butterfly, tingling with chloroform, gives
up her sleep.

Legs spread, the skeleton a pin pierces.
Bloodless. Mounted

on styrofoam under my bed.
Cocooned in quilts, I am seven.

~~~~~~

My period kicks in
and I never kill again.

There is no canoodling
(consider all the cadavers)

and I am too old
for lots that are empty.

I have areolae
to twiddle

~~~~~~

and an urge to dwell.

The forest oozes on my hair,
acorns whisking my feet.
Paper birch appeals, the rest is scruff.

At the shore, sand slips in my eyes,
nowhere to cheat the waves,
the ocean a relentless tongue.

In the jungle, moths the size of my face.
How beautiful I would be,
there among the monstrous.

In the desert, no closets.  No minis,
no thongs.  Just yucca,
and trees that taste like gingerbread.

~~~~~~

In the end, I sleep again
among dead wings.

One ever-after is this kingdom
of dustballs and weeds.

I clear the plot, erect a temple,
and stir the poison:

*I am loved, I can be loved.*

In the smoke, passion drifts.
Passion shimmers

with teeny tiny flutterings as if
it might be you.

## When Backlit

Hips tilted and legs apart, a much younger pose.
My gestures gather many shadows, each a fantasy of willingness.

If as cold as you say, how am I more indigo than mineral?
There is a glow to my eclipse, there is a side fully revealed.

I am everything when backlit.
Begging, explicit, monstrous.

Fiercer than you think, at my deepest, where atoms rub raw.
Which is one reason for writing instead of killing the light.

Dark words in a lap dance on white paper,
my dark mouth whistling the frozen sky.

Even sharpest ice on the grayest day is a knot of glint.
This could be the night to insist desire into my body.

All this time, I was never truly young.
All the ways to yield that are also ways to be sorry.

## Killer Selfies

What wild motive, the trembling red lip
of a volcano, she scores both climb and core,

she plants herself on the edge, undoubted.
What will not appear despite the tech:

blistering heat, a softening underfoot.
Her face is sequence.  It is all unstable,

the rim and ground, liquid as cream,
and backdrop seemingly.  The most she

would be, in sepia or vintage, her choice.
It requires footing.  Which she will lose.

\*


A snake coiled on the path, rising from sand,
that tiny brain, one motive for its stacked bones.

What filter to face down such poison?
Mock horror with incisors blazing, chin cock.

Would the click of the stick catch the sting?
X a cut in the arm.  X a pouty parting.

\*


A golden bridge, drowned in clouds, how
wind grabs my tresses, hence the choke.

No one really looks that pert.  Shopped, brushed.
It makes me unsafe, all the selves you can like.

My best—what if it happens only at the brink?
Here is my killer version, already live, down-

loaded, while my lesser cannot balance the rail.

## When Wolf

She below the rock cairns, a brooding wind, climbs higher.
She with a visceral pace, its bright shards of hunger.

She that savors hunger, gnawing emptiness as a recitation.
She that mangles her foot to cheat the metal hold.

She grunting at births that press her to the cold stone.
She panting at the edge of the pack, pursued by heavy clouds.

She night-bound, her howls what the moon hauls.
She loose in her pelt, what a moon lacks.

She lone, snapping off branches, beating the wind.
She that grips snow in her teeth, grinds it to rain.

She warm-mouthed, full of harm.
She that should be nothing but harm.

Up the slope, rattling stones loud enough to become prey.
Matted and wild. A huntress, a bitch.

She rear-mounted, standing on ice under his weight.
She stone-still, lasting.

## Blow

The forest voices a rustle through
the necklace
of the swing.  Blow, backdrop, blow.

As if conqueror, a quiet fever,
the terror of April
is everywhere:  metal rings dangle

from worn screws in the wood,
a moan
twisting on chains.  In my hands

a coupling, two blades
of grass,
creased fold over fold to the tips.

For what battle does grass shoulder
such sharpness?
Where do I set what I have torn?

My mind at war in a country
at war, unable
to un-mouth air into the meadow.

At its edges, branches snap, fall,
and
the swing shifts:  I wonder why

sparrows never ride.  On and on,
wind blows,
an assault among voices,

links or holes in the chain.

**When Original**
*Owen and Wagner Collection, Hood Museum of Art*

Ecstatic.  Ochres lap and enlarge, a complete account.
A plain of circles, rain-holes in the desert that sustain time.

Chalked on string bark, a fish.  A hunter smaller than the fish's tooth.
A yellow line licks the circles, an ancient act, dropped in a song.

Folded dunes:  vastness which is seamless which circles the room.

Here I am, blinking away charcoal, blanking a skin.

Would be berries, fragile with hue, could ink a bird's view.
Dreams are birds, hovering under the blue, riding slips and mists from holes.

I am not a bird.  The circles are severed heads.

The I sinks in the desert, past knees, then nipples, over a crown of hair.
Water on the wall, dream-barbs at the brush-tip, rain sliding over eyes.

The canvas relentless.  One touch and I am through.

## While She Was Spinning

'Twas the sleep of butter and lard,
        one hundred winters

         for rendering
the dead things, mittens and mince.

Stolid eon of flightlessness,
        how long

        and often
the stooks lay retting in fields,

only the yellow best for scutching.
        No use for royal,

        sky-hued
flowers or glaucous, veined leaves.

Nor the brown seeds, almost bitter,
        pips of apples,

        with none
of the sugar and gloss. She drooped

through the hackling: flax into linen,
        into money,

        cigarettes,
tea bags.  Dear Guests, hers was

never a fairy tale, though pricked
        she was by the wheel

        (splinter as soporific),
her whetted world picked up and

carried off.  All those minutes
        measured

               by boiling the water.
Dun-colored thread and basket, her

motive no more or less than labor,
        equal to the pinched

        weight of stone
walls.  Guests, she has been spent

dully.  Root for the moon nursing
        at her fingers,

        its unwary mouth
rouses her, working the sliver free.

## The Girl in the Cupboard

A cupboard is faithful, a six-sided breath.

There are slats in the door where sunlight demurs,
its radiance sliced like an egg;

where moonlight
angles its pale yen through my hair.

Wafts of pollen and mayflies and cocoa and electricity,
blameless as air.

Here is a dress swinging
from the neck, hem brushing the floor,
not enough to survive.

I pull clothes off their hangers and straddle
the silk cascade.

I ride the way my mind mounts
my body, spur and rope.

Dogs are out there,
sniffing the globe and the rank glove it wears.

Your dogs, searching, noses blowing snot and muck,
salting my wounds.

As a dog, I would never wag, such elation in my ass.

I will not come out.  You will not come in.

# TWO

## The History of Mothers of Sons

All sons sleep next to mothers, then alone, then with others
Eventually, all our sons bare molars, incisors
Meanwhile, mothers are wingless things in a room of stairs
A gymnasium of bars and ropes, small arms hauling self over self

Mothers hum nonsense, driving here
and there (Here! There!) in hollow steeds, mothers reflecting
how faint reflections shiver over the road
All the deafening musts along the way

Mothers favor the moon—hook-hung and mirroring the sun—
there, in a berry bramble, calm as a stone

This is enough to wrench our hand out of his
and simply devour him, though he exceeds even the tallest grass

Every mother recalls a lullaby, and the elegy blowing through it

# Vows

*The Macaque and the Dove*

What humbles the island is fire not water.
Wings crumple in the treetops.

A tiny hand, not human but akin to it,
combs flight from the plumage,
her damp shrine.  The dove
pleats, settles like a ship,

and the macaque worships
her body, steeped with blue.

*The time is plenty for breakage,*
(her eye haloed, his fur bracelets),
the pair embracing on the table
until they quit without a hitch.


*The Owl and the Greyhound*

The tongue of a wagger licks
the mouth-bone of the owl.

*Any mouth is plenty.*
Beak and teeth are devoted.

The hound's ribs dropkicked,
the owl whacked with a wheel,

there is no inversion more
than a beast boxed to a pulp.

The owl bitsy, the dog slobbering.
Her frills are badass.

His speed is bleak wisdom.
*This is no time for whispers.*

*The Python and the Hamster*

His keepers call him Repast.
Her coiled muscle ekes out a repose.
It takes courage to bow

to a mouthpiece in silence.  He honors us.
She grips him like faith,
not bread, and starves.

The serpent is a chain of haloes.
The rodent a dirty gnaw.

To be swallowed whole is love.
And a promise not to keep.

## When Coleoptera

Bewildered path beneath bark, the intricate tunneling of beetles.
A thin fate, between sheath & heart, no ground or sky.
Tree peelings in hand, the insect runes I stroke with my tongue.

My next self is invertebrate, hard-cased & flickering.
Working apart pith with heavy mandibles,
hindrances dissolve, a trail of pincer work & scuttle.

Only wood in my way.

Our dark bodies in lightless, voiceless lines.
The tiniest minds:  one consuming thought & such simple nights.

What persistence to inhabit, my exact shape & form, as if armor.
Already the iridescent carapace hardens under my wince.

Just in time, for a bird on the branch is tapping the tree.
And I am pinned to the only desire I know.

## Allium

Look to the allium, and not another word
about the son.  An ekphrastic, then: ecstatic,
romantic:  look to arched green, climbing hoods

of narcissus, drying to paper.  Look to umbrels,
sphered violet, a star formation over pursed angels,
prudish knots in a spread of leaves.

Not another word about him, or his mind,
like water rising over rocks,
or rocks sitting in water:  there it is, the trouble

that might be nature.  Look at the allium

and steady yourself:  night cracks through
the window overhead, all those cries echoing
from woods to sheets, and back.  Not another word

about mothers, yours or his:  you kneel
as a wife, pruning the leafless base of the allium.
Look past this bed, to encroaching brush, and rip

weed after weed to spare the allium.
Look to brown pods where petals crimp, pinch
them so the bulbs gorge.

**When Alpine**

There is life among the rocks.
Ochre lichen flakes like scales on a collapsed fish.
Raptors circle the nearest flinch.
Fireweed and lodgepole feather out of recent ash.

Seared trunk-bones, the slope in a deep exhaustion.
Frost, wedged between rocks, drips into bright crevasses.
Tarns, ink-pots, run-off, what grinds through granite.
Bluest sky, bluest ice:

the eras are deep vaults, peeking and seeping beyond.
And the ridge line is the skyline is pure water.
Glaciers are bitter, unsurvivable.
Forces that are understood but unbelievable.

The seas push up into air, tiny fish-bones against the clouds.
At the rim, the immensity of my son, breaking sticks, salt in his hair.

## Lay Down in the Garage with a Gun

Woe to the granite path,
slabs wider than your stride.

Woe the pebble eyes that pills
keep dry, and gravel

between thighs—why,
when desire drives dreams

like a herd, stumbling
through the wet field?

Spring snow burns the apple's
tight pink knots.  Into dirt

soaks your breath, on all fours,
yanking weeds out—

you would choke your heart
if you could reach the root.  Where

is a tree to climb, high enough
to crave a stone?

Your temples ache as the meadow
stares back, a far wall of green.

You only imagine a gun
that gets that ache.  Woe that gun

is just a word, heavy enough
to plummet down pages

and screw sorrow
to a chair, your lines keening

and arching on the desk.
Woe that your silence

was not louder or heard.
Where are last words,

in repose among all others,
a page you were writing,

that could be left,
and then found?

## How We Were at the End of Winter

*One*

Can you take measure
of the fence I will need?

Too soon, you say,
start with warmth
in a southern window.

Small seed cups on sills
never produced before,
but this winter fill
with leaflets, twisting
to face the light
over the cold beds.

I need more windows.

The end of winter
is a glint
on the snowman's
melting heart,
lumped on the grass.

I use daylight
as a vague blue shadow,

and our night
windows as both glass
and mirror,
my reflection
poured out over snow.

*Two*

Every question is a stone forced into my mouth,
the pressure brings tears to my eyes.

Days of melting, then more flakes fall.
Stuttering, the weather in our shutters and hair.

It is winter, my mouth opens in spring.  Like a screen door,
or a pond edge where the frogs freeze in their skin.

That first blink after thaw, how an orange eye waters
and burns, how warmth is what to fear while frozen.

All winter, in so many layers I cannot be touched,
while the pond rustles in its bed, clipping at the glaze.

A horned owl carries the frog in flight, tiny heart a tick
against the tongue, while wings fix the wind.

My fingers shiver, unhooked from their strings.
Numbness that is solace, a tightening of the world.

## Wintering

Cows in snow, stock-still and chilled to the skull,
grassless at the bell.  Vain reverie of the frozen,

dreams of lifting one leg towards another, hide to hide,
tails switching flanks—immediacy a mutual ice-field,

with a view to Cube and Cardigan, this cow dream.
I force sleep for any version of closeness:

pressed shuffle of rumps, moans and snorts of steam.
I force dreams while awake, snow-matted and squinting,

wide gaps in the herd that flood with visions:
over snow will drift the one missing all winter.

## When Crow

That I could be a shiny thing, spruce
laced with tinsel that drops its needles.

The spruce does not know it has died.
Standing in water on a tightened prong,

bluffing in the window, so drivers ogle
this hint at what joy can be.  What can

joy be?  Along the river, farms of X-
mas trees sown in rows of fog. An X

is Christ the way one crow is sorrow,
two crows are joy, and so on.  I refuse

promises from crows, harbingers
and scavengers already mar my days.

I struggle to right the spruce, pruned tip
of a larger thought, roots left behind, so

all I haul are hints.  Draping the tines
with baubles, wistful tokens.  What

careful regret will I place below?  Crows
peck the shimmering snow, what they

find is nested and strange.  No believer,
I still count crows.  Not shiny, I find joy.

**Lisa Furmanski** is a physician, specializing in geriatrics, and living in New Hampshire with her husband and sons. Her poetry has appeared widely, including work in *Poetry, Beloit Poetry Review, Prairie Schooner, Gettysburg Review, Hunger Mountain, Massachusetts Review, Denver Quarterly, Antioch Review, Tupelo Quarterly*, and elsewhere. Her poems have appeared on both *Poetry Daily* and *Verse Daily*. She has written a memoir/essay, *Two Bodies in a Room*, about the emotional landscape of doctoring, and is a certificate candidate in Narrative Medicine at Columbia University. Her work can be found at *lisafurmanski.com*.